MW01233026

Studies On The Ophioglossaceae

revision. There must therefore for the present be some doubt as to the proper nomenclature of some of the forms considered in this paper.

THE GAMETOPHYTE.

The first discovery of the gametophyte of the Ophioglossaceae was made by Hofmeister (Abh. d. k. sächs. Gesellsch. d. Wiss., 1857, pp. 657—662) who, in 1854, found the gametophyte of *Botrychium Lunaria* and two years later Mettenius (Filices Horti Botanici Lipsiensis, Leipzig, 1856, p. 119) described much more fully the gametophyte of *Ophioglossum pedunculosum*, which was cultivated in the botanical garden at Leipzig. No further additions were made to the subject until the writer (Structure and Development of Mosses & Ferns, 1st edit, 1895, pp. 224 – 228) succeeded in obtaining the first germinating stages of *O. pendulum* collected in the Hawaiian Islands, and those of *Botrychium virginianum*; and the older gametophyte of the later species was also described. In 1898 Jeffrey (The Gametophyte of *Botrychium virginianum*, University of Toronto Studies, 1898) published a complete account of the gametophyte and embryo of *Botrychium virginianum*. The latest contributions to the subject have been those of Lang (On the *Prothalli* of *Ophioglossum pendulum* and *Helminthostachys zeylanica*, Ann. ot Bot., XVI, pp. 23--56, 1902) who has described the gametophyte of *O. pendulum* and of *Helminthostachys*; and the still more recent papers of Bruchmann (Über das Prothallium und die Sporenpflanze von Botrychium Lunaria, Flora, XCVI, pp. 203—227, 1906; Über das Prothallium und Keimpflanze von *O. vulgatum*, Bot. Zeit, 1904). The latest contribution to the subject is a preliminary paper by Lyon (A New Genus of Ophioglossaceae, Bot. Gaz., XL, pp. 455—458, 1905) on the embryo of *B. obliquum*.

About six weeks in January and February of 1906 were spent by the writer in Ceylon. The greater part of the time was passed in the botanical gardens of Peradeniya, but an excursion was also made to the Barawa Forest. The Barawa Forest is not

very far from Colombo, near Hanwella, where LANG secured
his material of Ophioglossum and Helminthostachys. A week
or more was also spent at the mountain garden of Hakgala and
in the vicinity. *O. pendulum* was found to be fairly abundant
near Hanwella, but the weather was very dry, so that the
masses of humus in which the plants were growing were dry
as powder and no prothallia could be procured. However, an
abundance of ripe spores was secured, from which latter were
reared a number of small prothallia. In the low forest near
Hanwella, which is subject to regular inundations, *Helminthostachys zeylanica* was very abundant, and a large number
of young plants still connected with the gametophyte were
obtained, but no young prothallia could be found. Near Hakgala
a medium-sized terrestrial species of Ophioglossum, possibly
O. reticulatum, was common, and a very small number of
prothallia with the attached sporophytes were discovered, but
not enough to make a detailed study possible. The same, or a
very similar species, grew naer Peradeniya, but no prothallia
were found.

On reaching Buitenzorg it was noted that a small Ophioglossum was extremely common in the garden and elsewhere
in the neighborhood. This was considered to be *O. moluccanum*
SCHLECT., but it soon became evident that there were several
distinct forms, probably good species, growing together. Very
soon after arriving in Buitenzorg, sowings were made of this
species which, unlike the others that have been studied before,
was found to germinate very promptly, and repeated sowings
were made and the process of germination was carefully studied.
A number of older prothallia of this or a similar species was
found, and the most important details of its structure were
made out. The rare *O. intermedium* also occurs near Buitenzorg
and the earliest germination stages of this species also were
observed, but the amount of material was very small and no
complete study of the germination could be made. At Tjibodas,
the mountain station of the botanical garden, a species very
like the Ceylonese one was extremely abundant, but repeated

search failed to show any prothallia nor could the spores be made to germinate. *O pendulum*, which seems to be rare near Buitenzorg, was fairly common in the forest at Tjibodas, and of this species the writer secured a large number of prothallia in nearly all stages of development. A number of these were kept alive in closely stoppered bottles partly filled with the humus in which they were found, and at the present writing, -- December, 1906, — are still in good condition. A very fine lot of this species was seen in the botanical garden at Singapore, but there was not time to make a search for the prothallia which probably would have been found, as the conditions seemed very favorable. A species resembling *O. moluccanum* was also seen growing in the garden at Singapore.

GERMINATION IN O. MOLUCCANUM.

The extremely favorable conditions for plant growth at Buitenzorg indicated that here, if anywhere, germination experiments should succeed, and very soon after the writer's arrival a quantity of plants of *O. moluccanum* were secured and the spores were sown. As in all previous experiments with the Ophioglossaceae germination had been very slow, it was with much surprise that the first lot of spores sown, when examined a week later, were found to be germinating very freely and had evidently been growing for some days. New sowings were made, and in some cases the first germination stages were found within three days from the time the spores were sown. Inasmuch as the spores contained no chlorophyll, this rapid germination was quite unexpected. In the most favorable instances the greater part of the spores germinated, and many thousand germinating spores were seen, so that a very complete study could be made of the early phases of growth. The first sowings were made upon earth taken from where the plants were collected; the earth was placed in small glass dishes, and flooded with water. The spores were then scattered over the surface of the water, some sinking, but the greater part floating on the surface. In later experiments cavities were hollowed out in the earth and these were filled with water, while the rest of the earth was left wet, but not flooded. It was found that the spores germinated more promptly in the water than on the wet earth, and this suggested that probably in nature germination occurs where spores fall in slight depressions which could be filled with water for a time after heavy rains. The prothallia of Helminthostachys, — to judge from the locality where they were found in the Barawa Forest, — occurred only where the forest was subject to inundation, and it may be that free water is necessary for the germination of *O. moluccanum*, or at any rate facilitates germination. However, spores of Helminthostachys which were sown both on water and on earth could not be made to germinate. Spores of *O. moluccanum* sown later in a flower pot which was kept standing in water, but which was not flooded, did not germinate at all, or only showed very few germinating spores. The free prothallia found in Buitenzorg occurred in low ground between the projecting roots of trees where water might very well settle for some days in wet weather.

The spores of all the forms examined are of the tetrahedral type characteristic of other species of Ophioglossum, and the outer spore membranes are quite colorless, so that the spores appear either white or of a pale yellow tint. There was a marked difference in the size of the spores, and there was a difference in the surface sculpturings and the contents. An examination of the plants showed that at least two marked forms — probably distinct species — were present. One, probably the true *O. moluccanum* (Fig. 153), is somewhat smaller, with a pointed lanceolate sterile segment and medium-sized coarsely reticulate spores. The spores have dense granular contents with a considerable amount of starch as well as oil and albuminous granules. The other most striking form was usually somewhat larger, with cordate or nearly cordate sterile segment of the leaf, and decidedly larger, finely reticulate spores, more transparent and having little or no starch. Both of these types, however, showed great variability both in the size of the plant and the spores, and also to some degree a difference in the shape of the sterile segment. It is not unlikely that more than two species are present. As the different forms generally grew more or less mixed together, there was necessarily some doubt as to the identity of all specimens of germinating spores that were examined. It was found, however, that the coarsely reticulate spores, presumably belonging to the typical species, germinated more freely, and probably most of the germinating spores that were studied belong to this species. The largest spores came from the large cordate leaved form, but no success was had in germinating these.

The first sowings of the spores were made on March 13th. These were examined a week later, and a large part of them were found to be germinated, the young prothallia having two or even three cells. Sowings made on March 26th had begun to germinate three days later, and by March 31 showed many two-celled stages, and some which were doubtfully three-celled. The exospore bursts, as usual, along the three radiating lines of its ventral surface, and the enclosed endospore protrudes through the cleft, the three lobes of the exospore being forced widely apart. The projecting portion of the spore contents has somewhat less granular matter in it than the portion within the spore membrane, but it is not narrowed at all, and does not seem to be a proper rhizoid, as it never becomes elongated. Shortly after the bursting of the spore coat the projecting portion becomes shut off by a transverse wall (Fig. 2). The upper cell is somewhat smaller as a rule, and contains much less granular matter; but as already stated, it does not become elongated and while it is perhaps the equivalent of the first rhizoid of the leptosporangiate fern, it never assumes the form of a proper rhizoid. Owing to the dense cell contents, the large central nucleus of the fern is not very clearly discernable, although its position can be easily made out. The outer cell wall becomes more or less distinctly thickened.

Ordinarily the next division, as in *O. pendulum* (CAMPBELL

loc. cit., Fig. 109) is in the lower cell and divides it into two
cells, which are of unequal size (Figs. 5 and 6). The larger of
these may divide further into two nearly equal cells by a
vertical wall (Fig. 6) but no further divisions could be found
in the species.

Figure 8 gives two views of a young prothallium of four
cells showing their arrangement.

In *O. pedunculosum*, which may perhaps be identical with
some of our forms, METTENIUS found that the older prothallia
may develop chlorophyll under certain conditions, and a special
effort was made to determine whether there was any chlorophyll found in the earlier stages of germination of *O. moluccanum*. It was found that while in the ungerminated spore and
during the first stages of development no chlorophyll could be
detected, not infrequently a small amount ef chlorophyll was
formed in the three or four-celled prothallia. Not uncommonly
specimens were encountered in which there were one to three
distinct chromatophores of a pale, but unmistakable, green
color (Fig. 4). In one instance a number of specimens which
had been kept on a slide in a moist chamber for several days
showed chromatophores of a golden brown color, but the cause
of this could not be determined. The amount of chlorophyll
is evidently insufficient for the independent growth of the
young gametophyte, and after a few weeks or a month,
the granular contents have almost disappeared and many of
the young prothallia have the cells collapsed and are evidently dead.

In many of the cultures which were kept very wet a
Chytridium or some allied fungus attacked them and quickly
destroyed them. In another culture, a filamentous fungus was
seen, and at first was thought to be possibly the mycorhiza
which associates itself with the older prothallia. This fungus,
however, grew rapidly and soon destroyed the young prothallia,
which in no cases observed in this species, advanced beyond
the four-celled stage.

THE GERMINATION IN O. PENDULUM.

The earliest germination stages of *O. pendulum* were first found by the writer in 1892, when spores of this species were collected in the Hawaiian Islands and successfully grown up to a condition with three cells, but all efforts to carry them beyond this stage failed. It was decided to make new experiments, if possible, and to this end ripe spores were collected both in Ceylon (in the Barawa Forest and at Peradeniya) and in Java (at Tjibodas). The spores were sown on wet humus taken from the stratum where the plants were growing. This humus was kept in wide mouthed bottles, and these were successfully carried from Ceylon to Java, and some of them reached California in good condition.

Germination in this species is slow, and it was about a month before the first stages of germination were seen. Spores sown in Tjibodas on April 18th were first found germinating at Buitenzorg on May 24th, at this time germination being pretty well advanced. Some of these were still alive and in good condition in September, but have not been examined since. On June 3d a number of these had three cells. The germination in all cases corresponds exactly with the writer's former observations, and differs in no way from that in *O. moluccanum*. In no cases could any trace of clorophyll be seen, and apparently the prothallium of *O. pendulum* is strictly saprophytic throughout its existence.

A small amount of the rare *O. intermedium* was collected near Buitenzorg, and a few ripe spores were secured. These spores contained somewhat less dense contents than those of the two preceding species, and have a more delicate epispore. Spores were sown on March 30th in Buitenzorg, and when examined about weeks later no germinations were found, nor did a second examination, — about the end of April — show any further results. On May 21st, however, two 3-celled prothallia were found, and subsequently a small number of others, but no later stages were discovered. These young prothallia appeared in every respect like the similar stages in the other species that were studied (Fig. 9).

In *O. moluccanum* none of the prothallia were found to contain more than four cells. These four-celled prothallia usually (Figs. 4—8) have the upper cells quite undivided, while the lower had the larger of the two original cells divided by a vertical wall into approximately equal parts. In this condition they remained until all the food material was exhausted. The cells became more and more transparent, and finally died — apparently from starvation.

In *O. pendulum*, however, a number of young prothallia were found which had increased very much in size and undergone further cell division. The first of these were observed on April 3d and had developed from spores sown in Peradeniya on February 9th; these had been brought to Buitenzorg. These young prothallia (Figs. 12 and 13) had from four to six cells. It was found that in each case the mycorhiza had connected itself with the young prothallium, and evidently had caused the stimulus in its growth. In every case where the young prothallium had more than three cells, there was found an association with the mycorhiza which could be easily seen to penetrate into the basal cell. The infection was in all cases due to fragments of mycelium, and in no cases to anything which could be interpreted as spores. The mycorhizal fungus was apparently growing free in the humus where the spores were sown. This soil had been taken from about the roots of the sporophytes which furnished the spores.

The free surface of the basal cell has its wall decidedly thickened, and it was here that the infection took place in all the specimens seen. The branching mycelium of the mycorhiza was closely applied to the surface of the cell, and a haustorium was sent down through the cell wall into the basal cell (Figs. 13 and 14). This haustorium is pointed at first, but after penetration into the cell its end enlarges and assumes the form of a somewhat thickened worm-shaped body, much thicker than the free mycelium outside. In the cell infected with the fungus, the contents show the peculiar aggregated appearance characteristic of the infected cells of the older prothallium. On April 6th a specimen with seven cells was found (Figs. 15 and 16). Observations on the further development of the prothallia were interrupted by a trip to Tjibodas, which lasted over a month. The cultures were left at Buitenzorg, and on my return in May observations were resumed. On May 24th several young prothallia were found, and on May 26th a number more. The largest of these had, as nearly as could be determined, thirteen cells. This was the largest number found in any of the young prothallia (Figs. 18—20).

These largest prothallia show that as in *O. moluccanum*, the divisions are mainly in the lower cell so that the apex of prothallium probably as in the true ferns develops in the lower of the two prothallial cells. The upper cell, however, also undergoes further divisions, and there is no very marked difference between the upper and lower ends of the prothallium. At this stage there is a marked resemblance, except for the absence of chlorophyll, to the early germination stages of *Lycopodium cernuum* (TREUB — Étude, sur les Lycopodiacées, Annales du Jardin Botanique de Buitenzorg IV, Pl. IX, Figs. 4—8). The mycorhiza penetrates the adjacent upper cells and in the cells so infected the contents quickly assume the characteristic aggregated appearance, while the apical region probably remains permanently free from the endophyte, as it does in the adult prothallium.

The number of young prothallia found was too small to make it possible to determine exactly what may be considered the normal succession of cell division, and whether at this early stage there is a definite apical cell could not be decided. As will be seen from the figures, there is evidently a good deal of variation in the early divisions. Fig. 20 shows the surface view of one of the largest specimens, with probably thirteen cells. Fig. 19 shows three optical transverse sections of the same. In these larger prothallia there is already the beginning of the axial tissue. Whether the cell x (Fig. 19) is to be regarded as the apical cell cannot be certainly determined.

Owing to the writer's departure from Java early in June, it was impossible to trace the development of prothallia further. This much, however, is certain — without the infection of the fungus, growth will not proceed beyond the three-celled stage, and apparently no chlorophyll will develop so that the prothallium from its earliest stage must be considered to be strictly saprophytic in its nutrition.

Whether the oval body described is to be considerad as a sort of tubercle, such as is found in *Lycopodium cernuum* mnst be decided by further investigations. Lang's descriptions and figures of the smallest specimens which he discovered would indicate that this is not the case in *O. pendulum;* but the tuberous body usually found in the older prothallia of *O. moluccanum* and *O. pedunculosum* — also in *O. vulgatum* — would indicate that in these species it is quite probable that a primary tubercle is first formed and subsequently the sexual branch.

THE ADULT GAMETOPHYTE.

The adult gametophyte is known in *O. pedunculosum* (Mettenius) *O. vulgatum* (Bruchmann) and in *O. pendulum* (Lang). The former species was described by Mettenius just fifty years ago. According to Raciborsky, *O. pedunculosum* Desv., is synonymous with *O. moluccanum* Schlecht., and the close resemblance between the prothallia of the latter species found by the writer and those described by Mettenius, make it probable that the specimens collected at Buitenzorg, at least most of them, really belong to *O. moluccanum*, although it is quite likely that some of them should be referred to one of the other species which grow associated with the true moluccanum. Mettenius' specimens appeared spontaneously in pots where the plants were cultivated in the Leipzig botanical gardens, and he described accurately the most important points of their structure. He was, however, unable to obtain germination of the spores.

Shortly after my arrival at Buitenzorg in March, 1206, finding *O. moluccanum* very common, search was made at once for the prothallia. Many small plants were found, which it was hoped might be attached to prothallia, but in nearly all cases these were found to be growing from fragments of roots, so common a phenomenon in most species of Ophioglossum. Diligent search in various parts of the garden, however, finally resulted in the discovery of a small number of prothallia, but these were all old and insufficient for showing clearly the character of the reproductive organs. Finally, however, on April 8th, between forty and fifty were found together, and although most of these had the sporophyte already developed, and no young reproductive organs present, still a small number of younger ones were secured, and these made it possible to determine the more important characters of the sexual organs. The young sporophytes were growing under a tree near the avenue of Ficus, the "Waringin Allee" in the park adjoining the botanical garden. A number of very small plants were seen growing in a sort of shallow basin enclosed by the roots of the tree, and on taking up some of these the attached gametophyte was discovered. Careful search through the earth revealed a number of prothallia, about a half dozen of which were still unfertilized, and these bore archegonia and antheridia. The prothallia were very small — much smaller than the prothallia of *O. pedunculosum*, as figured by METTENIUS. but otherwise they closely resembled them. They were also much smaller than the prothallia of *O. vulgatum* described by BRUCH-MANN. The basin-like space between the roots of the tree would be likely to hold water after heavy rain, and it is likely that this facilitates the germination of the spores, as in artificial cultures, since we have seen these germinated more readily when placed in water than those simply placed on moist earth. Most of these prothallia, as already stated, were very small, and were not buried very deeply — probably not more than 3 centimeters and sometimes less.

The prothallia are usually slender bodies, from $^1/_2$ to 1 cen-

timeter in length, and none of them were found to branch.
They showed a more or less conspicuous basal tuber like that
described by METTENIUS for *O. pedunculosum*, and indeed they
very closely resembled his figures of the simpler forms of that
species. He states, however, that the prothallia he examined
were very variable in size — from $1^1/_2$ lines in length to 2
inches or more. About a month later the same locality was
visited, and a small number of prothallia were secured, but
all of these were old ones. Two or three were found in the
garden, but these were also too old to show the young archegonia and antheridia. The youngest specimen found (Fig. 33)
showed a small irregular tuberous body of a brownish color,
from which the white appendage or branch extended. The older
ones also showed the basal tuber, but the cylindrical branch
was much longer (Fig. 21). The tuber was brownish in color,
as were the older parts of the branch, but the tip was white,
ond this gradually passed into the pale brown of the basal
parts. Owing to their slender form the prothallia were not always readily distinguishable from the roots, and in some cases
a microscopic examination was necessary before their real
nature could be certainly determined. Growing from the surface are scattered short brown hairs like those described by
METTENIUS for *O. pedunculosum*. These, according to BRUCHMANN,
are quite absent from the prothallia of *O. vulgatum*. Archegonia and antheridia are formed at an early period, and can
be traced to the base of the fertile branch, or in some cases
may be found even upon the tuber. In most of the specimens
found at Buitenzorg, the reproduction organs were produced
in much smaller numbers than is the case either in *O. pedunculosum* or *O. vulgatum*. Among the specimens found, however,
was one (Fig. 23) very much larger than any of the others,
and this had very large numbers of old archegonia. It is highly
probable that this represents the second species, but unfortunately there was no way of determining to which of the two
or three species associated under the name *O. moluccanum* it
belonged.

Some of the specimens were fixed with one per cent chromic
acid, others with acetic alcohol (alcohol 90 % — acetic
acid 10 %). These were then imbedded in paraffine in the
usual way, and a series of sections made. The material fixed
with chromic acid gave especially satisfactory results. The
sections were stained with a double stain of aniline safranine
and gentian violet.

Of the very small number of young prothallia obtained, the
one shown in Figure 43 was best. The basal part was a bulb-
like tuber from which extended the delicate slender branch
which bore the reproductive organs. The cells of the tuber and
the lower part of the branch showed the characteristic endophytic fungus, but the greater part of the branch is quite free
from this, and the cells appear almost transparent, but they
contain numerous small starch granules. The endophyte is
found in considerable quantities in the cells of the tuber
(Fig. 50). The hyphae, which stained quite strongly with the
gentian violet, are irregular in outline, and branch freely. Not
infrequently branches can be seen piercing the cell wall of the
adjacent cells. The nuclei of the infested cells appear quite
normal, but there are usually present strongly staining irregular clumps of which it is hard to say whether they are
parts of the fungus or merely aggregates of the protoplasm
of the prothallial cells such as are easily discernable in *O. pendulum*. This endophyte was much more apparent in some of
the larger prothallia found, which may have belonged to some
other species than the one under consideration.

In the living condition the pointed apex of the prothallium
is pure white, and even with a hand lens the projection of
the antheridium is clearly evident. METTENIUS noticed this
"varicose" appearance of the smaller prothallia. A median
section (Fig. 43) shows the decidedly pointed end with a clearly
defined apical cell closely resembling BRUCHMANN's figures of
O. vulgatum. Owing to the very small amount of material
available, no satisfactory transverse section of the apex could
be made, and it is not possible to state whether the apical

cell in transverse section is three-sided, as in *O. vulgatum* (which is most likely) or four-sided, as in *O. pendulum* In the specimens under consideration antheridia were more numerous than archegonia, although several of the latter were present. The antheridia arise, in general, in acropetal succession, but it is' likely that secondary ones may be formed among the older ones; at least, this seems to be true. The archegonia are scattered among the antheridia without any definite order. In some specimens examined — especially in the larger forms shown in Figure 23 — old archegonia were formed in great numbers, many more than antheridia. In some of the specimens examined, however, a great part of the prothallium was quite destitute of either archegonia, or antheridia, and in this respect they differ markedly from any of those figured by METTENIUS or BRUCHMANN for *O. pedunculosum* or *O. vulgatum*.

All of the specimens collected at Buitenzorg showed a greater or lesser number of rhizoids both at the base and along the fertile branch (Figs. 25—26). In the more slender forms, however, these rhizoids were few. They were in some cases two-celled (Fig. 53) but usually consisted of a single elongated cell (Fig. 52). Not uncommonly there could be seen within the penetrating filament of the mycorhiza (Fig. 51) as has been described for other species of *Ophioglossum*, as well as for *Botrychium* and *Helminthostachys*. The rhizoids are much longer relatively than in *O. pendulum*, and the two-celled ones resemble somewhat the multicellular hairs found in *Botrychium*. According to BRUCHMANN, the rhizoids are quite absent from the prothallia of *O. vulgatum*. The endophyte is most abundant in the tuber, but extends into the branch, where it occupies the layer outside of the axial tissue which remains nearly or quite free from the endophyte. According to METTENIUS, the prothallia often grow above the surface of the earth, when they become more or less flattened and sometimes divided into several small lobes. In such cases chlorophyll is developed, but METTENIUS was unable to note any further development of these green lobes. BRUCHMANN also demonstrated the development of chlorophyll in *O. vulgatum* when the prothallia were exposed to the light, but did not observe any flattening of the apex. Owing to the very small number of active prothallia found by the writer, he was unable to test the power of developing chlorophyll in *O. moluccanum*. In one case a prothallium was found in the garden at Buitenzorg growing almost at the surface of the ground. There appeared to be a very small amount of chlorophyll in this, but it was not certain that such was really the case. The occasional appearance of chromatophores in the germinating spores harmonizes with the capacity of the older prothallia to develop chlorophyll under the stimulation of light.

The small size of the prothallia and the cessation of growth after the sporophyte is formed indicates that the gametophyte lives only for one season, which is probably the case also in *Helminthostachys*. In this respect *O. moluccanum* and its allies differ markedly from *O. pendulum* and *O. vulgatum*, where the gametophyte may live for many years.

At Hakgala, in Ceylon, an undetermined species of *Ophioglossum* of the type of *O. reticulatum* was common. A careful search finally brought to light a small number of prothallia (Figs. 30—31) which resembled closely those of *O. moluccanum*, and the young sporophyte is also of the same type. The material was too scanty to make a further study possible, but from the external appearance it is likely that its structural details would closely resemble those of *O. moluccanum*.

LANG (loc. cit.) discovered the prothallia of *O. pendulum* in the Barawa Forest reserve in Ceylon, and the writer visited the same locality. Although large masses of the older sporophyte were found, they grew high up on the branches of trees and it was difficult to remove the mass of humus in which they were growing, as it was excessively dry and fell to pieces. If any prothallia were present they must have been completely dried up. At any rate, careful search through such of the humus as could be secured yielded no results. In the botanical garden at Singapore a fine growth of the plant was found attached to the stem of a species of Phoenix. There was no time for making an examination, but from his later studies in Java the writer is inclined to think that prothallia were probably present.

In the forest at Tjibodas, however, after considerable search, the prothallia were finally discovered in several places, and a large number of specimens was procured, so that a thorough study was possible. The result of this study is a confirmation of LANG's investigations, but it was possible to extend these observations in several respects, — notably, the spermatogenesis and the development of the embryo, the latter being a point which especially needed investigation. In all cases the prothallia discovered were found in the humus packed between the old leaf bases of *Asplenium Nidus*. LANG collected his material in the humus about *Polypodium quercifolium*. It is very evident that the prothallia are very long lived, as they were found deeply buried in the humus between the old leaf bases some thirty or forty centimeters below the living crown of leaves, and these old leaves must have been dead many years. Presumably the spores fall between the upper leaves of the Asplenium and sift down between them into the humus at their bases where the spores germinate. They are gradually buried deeper and deeper with the accumulating humus as the leaf bases are pushed further and further down by the development of the new leaves at the crown of the plant. The mass of humus in a large plant of *A. Nidus* must weigh at least 25 kilogrammes, and it was between the older leaf bases that most of the specimens were collected. The branches of the prothallia were often much flattened by the pressure of the leaf bases between which they were lying, but except for this, growth takes place in all directions. BRUCHMANN states that in *O. vulgatum* the prothallia are also very long lived, probably often living for ten years or more, and this is also the case in *Botrychium virginianum*. Helminthostachys on the other hand, as already stated, is probably annual like *O. moluccanum*.

In searching for the prothallia of *O. pendulum* one naturally looked for small sporophytes which might be attached to the buried gametophyte, but the smallest leaves seen reached a length of 10 centimeters or more, and had not at all the aspect of belonging to germ plants. These in all cases were found to grow from a tuberous body attached to the buried roots. However, when the humus in which these were growing — which was packed tightly between the broad persistent leaf bases of the fern — was examined, in a number of cases the prothallia were found. In one instance several hundred were collected from one large plant of *Asplenium Nidus*. In no cases, however, was the leafy bud growing directly from the gametophyte. The prothallia closely resemble LANG's figures and descriptions, but are in many cases very much larger and more extensively branched than any of the specimens collected by him in Ceylon. In strong contrast to the prothallium of *O. moluccanum*, the gametophyte of *O. pendulum* is extensively branched. It often forms a somewhat stellate mass, but is usually very irregular in form (Figs. 34—42). The branches penetrate in all directions between the dense tangle of roots which the Asplenium sends into the humus between the persistent leaf bases, and on pulling back these leaf bases a mass of fine humus is held together by the mat of roots and can be removed intact. The prothallia are excessively brittle, and it is practically impossible to remove the large ones without a loss of some of the numerous branches. These break off and no doubt naturally serve to propagate the gametophyte, which apparently is capable of unlimited growth in this way. It is often impossible to say whether the smaller ones that are found loose in the humus are anything more than branches which have become spontaneously separated from the larger ones. A small number of living specimens were brought back to America in masses of the humus, kept moist in stoppered bottles, and these have grown and are in a perfectly normal and healthy condition at the present time.

The older parts of the gametophyte are dark brown in color, but the tips of the branches are white, as in *O. moluccanum*.

The branching is very irregular and old fragments kept moist often send out great numbers of adventitious buds. (Fig. 39) which probably in time develop into normal branches.

Figures 34—38 show a number of the commoner forms. Figure 34 represents the largest one met with. This is by no means complete, as a number of branches were unavoidable broken off in removing it from among the tangle of roots in which it was imbedded. This measures about 15 millimeters in diameter — more than twice the size of the largest specimen secured by LANG. It is also very much more extensively branched and considerably flattened by pressure. The surface of the older parts of the prothallia shows a slightly roughened appearance due to the numerous very short papillate hairs which occur abundantly upon it. They are never of the slender pointed form found in *O. moluccanum*. The empty antheridia are very conspicuous, and appear as light brown spots readily seen with the naked eye. (Figures 35—36). The branching is in some cases dichotomous, but lateral branches may arise at almost any point, and old fragments of the prothallia, as already indicated, often develop many adventitious buds. BRUCH- MANN describes somewhat similar buds in *O. vulgatum*. It is seen that the form of prothallia is thus exceedingly variable. The rate of growth of the prothallia kept by the writer, as well as their position in the humus about the plant, indicate that they are very long lived, and as has already been indicated, the ready separation of branches which thus form new individuals practically makes the duration unlimited.

In the preparation of the material collected it was fixed partly with 1º/₀ chromic acid and partly with FLEMMING's weak solution. Both methods gave good results and no difficulty was experienced in making excellent preparations of the repro- ductive organs and embryo. The same double stain of gentian violet and safranine was employed as in the case of *O. mo- luccanum*.

The arrangement of the tissues in the prothallium of *O. Pendulum* is much the same as in *O. moluccanum*, but all the parts are on a larger scale. The rhizoids (Fig. 48) are, as LANG showed, much shorter, but more numerous than in any other species. The endophyte is also much more conspicuous and was studied somewhat carefully. In the youngest parts of the prothallium it is absent, but in the older portions it is very apparent and conspicuous. Occasionally, fragments of the fungus were found on the outside of the prothallium, and evidently the same form as those observed infecting the very young prothallia which arise from the germinating spores. These hyphæ appeared in some cases to have an occasional septum, and this was also the case in the mycorhiza which infects the young prothallium. In all of the mycelia within the prothallium septa appeared to be quite absent. An infection of the prothallium through the rhizoids was seen in a number of cases, and corresponds to the account given by LANG and BRUCHMANN for the species examined by them. An examination of the young cells before the invasion of the fungus (Fig. 55) shows a conspicuous nucleus and numerous starch grains which stain very strongly with gentian violet. The invading mycelium, whether from the outside of the prothallium or from adjacent cells, penetrates the cell wall and ramifies within the cell. Apparently the growth, as JEFFREY found in the endophyte of *Botrychium virginianum*, is entirely intracellular. The hyphæ are noticeably thicker than those of the external mycorhiza.

In material treated with chromic acid the endophyte was perfectly fixed, and stained sharply with the double stain, the walls assuming a violet color and the numerous nuclei staining deep red with the safranine. In the younger hyphæ, which are of varying size, the protoplasm is densely granular, but in the older ones the granular appearance disappears to a considerable extent, but the nuclei continue to stain strongly. JEFFREY has made a careful study of the endophyte in *Botrychium virginianum*, and except for its larger size, that found in *O. pendulum* (which has also been studied by LANG) agrees closely with his account. As in other cases observed, the fungus is quite variable. Sometimes (Fig. 58) the filaments are nearly straight, running from cell to cell and branching sparingly. Sometimes (Fig. 56) a cell is completely filled with a dense tangle of hyphæ, while in other cases there are sack-like swellings of very irregular form (Fig. 57). Not infrequently quite regular, nearly globular, bodies are seen, recalling the young oögonia of the Peronosporeae (Fig. 59). They at first contain comparatively few nuclei scattered through the reticulately arranged cytoplasm. In the older ones the nuclei are very numerous and decidedly larger (Fig. 61). It looked in some cases as if this was a preparation for the formation of spores, but no certain evidence of the discharge of such spores could be seen, although in several instances there was an appearance noted which might point to this — masses of nuclei apparently free in the cell of the host. Structures resembling the "conidia" described by JEFFREY for Botrychium (loc. cit. p. 12) were seen and were probably the same thing. In most of the cells infested by the fungus was noted the peculiar aggregated appearance so frequently described (Fig. 56). Here it is clear that the irregular clumps are formed by the aggregation and breaking down of the starch granules found in the young cells. The nucleus of the host cell appears to be little affected by the growth of the fungus, and can usually be found quite unchanged even in those cells which are almost completely filled by the endophyte.

The endophyte, as in the other forms that have been studied, is quite absent from the apical region of the branches. In the old tissues of the gametophyte it is often present in great abundance. There is a more or less well marked zone inside the superficial tissue where the fungus is especially abundant (Figs. 45—46), while the central region is quite free from the fungus or only slightly infested. However, the limits of the infested zone are not very clearly marked, and any cell of the older tissue of the gametophyte may harbor the fungus.

159

THE APICAL GROWTH.

Lang found that the apical cell in the *O. pendulum* was a four-sided pyramid, and not tetrahedral, as in *O. vulgatum*; the writer's observations confirm this. In longitudinal section (Figs. 47—68) the apical cell appears triangular with a fairly regular segmentation, but there is also active division in the adjacent tissue and apparently the segmentation of the apical cell is not very rapid. Cross sections show the apical cell to be approximately four-sided (Fig. 67), but the sides are not always of equal length, and occasionally it is almost triangular in outline. Possibly it may be that in some cases, as in *O. vulgatum*, it is tetrahedral. There seems to be no absolute rule, however, as to the succession of divisions in the young segments. A more or less definite superficial layer arises from the first periclinal divisions, but anticlinals succeed rapidly.

THE SEXUAL ORGANS.

There is much difference in the time of the appearance of the sexual organs. Sometimes there are none at all near the apex, while in some instances the young sexual organs can be recognized in the second youngest series of segments (Fig. 68). The mother cells of the young archegonia and antheridia are much alike, and it is not easy to distinguish them apart in their earliest phases. The mother cell is cut out by a series of vertical intersecting walls in the outer cell of the young segment. While in a general way the young reproductive organs arise in acropetal succession there may also develop later intercalary ones. The number is often very great, but sometimes they are formed rather sparingly; although both archegonia and antheridia are usually mingled somewhat indiscriminately, it is not uncommon for one or the other to predominate and some branches may be almost exclusively devoted to the formation of antheridia. The latter are very large, — probably larger than in any other Pteridophyte, and are easily visible to the naked eye.

THE ANTHERIDIUM.

The antheridium of Ophioglossum has been figured by MET-
TENIUS, BRUCHMANN and LANG. It closely resembles that of the
eusporangiate ferns, and also is much like that of Equisetum
and Lycopodium. As in all of these, it is sunk deeply in the
tissue of the prothallium, only the opercular cell and its imme-
diate neighbors being free. While very young it lies flush with the
neighboring cells of the prothallium, but later may become
more or less elevated above the surface forming a low promi-
nence which in slender prothallia like those of *O. moluccanum*
may give an irregular outline to the branch which bears them
(Fig. 43). In *O. pendulum* this is less marked, but in this
species also there may be a decided projection of the ripe
antheridium. The first division in both archegonium and antheridium is periclinal and separates the primary cover cell from
the inner cell which in the antheridium, by further division,
gives rise to the spermatocytes. All the species appear to
agree closely in the development of the antheridium. There is
more or less variation in the form of the mother cell which
is sometimes comparatively broad and shallow (Figs. 62—70),
sometimes deep and narrow (Fig 68). In the latter case the
primary cover cell is deeper relatively than in the former. Of
the two primary cells the inner one is larger and has a correspondingly large nucleus, but otherwise there is little difference
between them. Very soon, however, the protoplasm of the inner
cells becomes more granular.

The first division in the inner cell is not always the same.
BRUCHMANN does not state what its position is in *O. vulgatum*,
and my material of *O. moluccanum* was too scanty to determine
whether the vertical position shown in Figure 63 is constant
or not. LANG states that he found this to be regularly the case
in *O. pendulum*, and the writer has frequently found this to
be true in that species, but not uncommonly the first wall in
the inner cell of the antheridium may be transverse (Fig. 68).
The second walls intersect the first at right angles, and there

are always four nearly equal inner cells resulting (Fig. 72).
The third set of walls is vertical, and the next in some cases
at least (Fig. 73) is in the same direction. This is not true, however, of the deeper and narrower type of antheridium (Fig. 68).
Further divisions continue until the number of spermatocytes
is very large. The fully developed mass of spermatocytes is
plainly visible to the naked eye, and in *O. pendulum* may
reach a diamater of more than 325 μ. More than 250 cells
can be counted in a single section of a large antheridium, and
this would mean that there are several thousand in the whole
antheridium, — probably more than in any other Pteridophyte.
In *O. moluccanum* (Figs. 64—65) the number is much smaller.
The antheridium of *O. vulgatum* appears to be intermediate in
size between that of *O. moluccanum* and *O. pendulum*. The
nucleoli which are conspicuous in the younger cells (Figs.
63—72) become less evident in the older ones. According to
METTENIUS (loc. cit. Figs. 18, 19) the outer wall of the antheridium is composed of two layers of cells, but LANG and
BRUCHMANN both found that the central part of this outer wall
is but one cell in thickness. The cover really is composed only
in part of the cells derived from the original cover cell, as
the mass of spermatocytes extends laterally far beyond the
limits of the cover cell, this being especially the case where
the mother cell is deep and narrow.

The first wall to be formed in the cover cell is nearly
median and vertical (Fig. 72) and this is followed by a second
wall which intersects it, as well as one of the lateral walls of
the primary cover cell, so as to include a nearly triangular
cell (Fig. 76). In the latter there are formed later, as both
BRUCHMANN and LANG showed, a varying number of segments
arranged spirally in the fashion of the segments of a three-
sided apical cell (Fig. 78). The same thing occurs in Lycopodium (TREUB-Études sur les Lycopodiacées, II, Annales du
Jardin Botanique de Buitenzorg. V, pl. XX, Fig. 6). The
Marattiaceae and Equisetum (CAMPBELL, loc. cit., 1st edit.
Fig. 221). The last-formed triangular cell is the opercular

cell (Fig. 78 o). From the prothallial tissue which adjoins the sperm cells are cut off flattened cells (Fig 64 m) which invest the sperm cells with a more or less definite layer of "mantle cells". The limits of the original cover cell are usually plainly visible in both longitudinal and surface sections (Figs. 77—78).

The material of *O. moluccanum* was not abundant enough to make a study of the living spermatozoids possible, and in *O. pendulum*, although repeated efforts were made to secure the opening of the antheridium and the discharge or the spermatozoids, they were all unseccessful, and just what the conditions are that are necessary for this must remain for the present unsettled. Apparently the development of the antheridium is excessively slow, and this perhaps accounts for the fact that none of the specimens selected for experiment seemed to have the stages ready for dehiscence. There is no reason to suppose that the method of dehiscence differs materially from that described by BRUCHMANN for *O. vulgatum* (loc. cit. p. 238). As in the latter species the opening is effected by the destruction of the triangular cell, which often, before opening, shows a discolored appearance — especially conspicuous in material fixed with the Flemming solution. The empty antheridium, in longitudinal section, shows the destroyed opercular cell very plainly, and the strongly projecting „mantle cells" surrounding the emply cavity. In no cases seen by the writer was the chambered appearance, due to the persistence of some of the primary cell walls such as is sometimes found in Botrychium, observed. (See MOSSES & FERNS, 2d edit., Fig. 128).

While the writer was unsuccessful in obtaining free spermatozoids, it was possible neverthelese to make a very satisfactory study of the spermatogenesis, for which *Ophioglossum* is especially suited, owing to the very large size of the spermatozoids. The spermatozoids of *O. pendulum* are probably the largest known among the Pteridophytes. *O. moluccanum* proved especially good for the purpose, but the small number of antheridia available made it impossible to secure all the stages.

This material was fixed with 1%, chromic acid and stained
with gentian violet and aniline safranine. The coloring thus
obtained was beautifully clear, and the blepharoplast stained
with extraordinary sharpness. The spermatozoids of *O. pendulum*
are even larger than those of *O. moluccanum*, and a very
satisfactory series of these was prepared, which has made
it possible to study practically all of the stages ot development. In the study of the spermatozoids in *O. pendulum* the
material was fixed with weak FLEMMING's solution and also
1% chromic acid. Both of these reagents fixed the material
satisfactorily. The nucleus was rather better stained in the
chromic acid preparations, as there was a tendency to over-
stain in the other material, but the blepharoplast and cilia
were much clearer in the material fixed with the FLEMMING
solution. In all cases the same double stain was employed.

If the sperm cells are examined previous to the final division
to form the spermatocytes (Figs. 79, 84) the nucleus will
usually show a small but distinct nucleolus and a dense reticulum. The whole stains strongly with safranine. The cytoplasm
is fairly dense, with granules of various kinds in it. In the
material fixed with FLEMMING's solution there are often small
black specks, perhaps fatty bodies, which sometimes interfere
somewhat with the study of the cytoplasm. In well stained
sections the blepharoplasts may be seen as two small rounded
bodies (b) lying near the nucleus. Several cases of the final
nuclear divisions were met with, but all of these were in
material fixed with chromic acid, and the blepharoplasts were
not very well differentiated (Fig. 85). The nuclear spindle is
very distinct, and the nuclear segments extraordinarily numerous.
Indeed, it was quite impossible to determine their number,
but the figures (85, 86) will show the very large nuclear plate.
The latter was often sectioned transversely so that the whole
number of segments could be seen (Fig. 86). The number of
chromosomes is evidently much greater than in the nuclei of
the younger antheridial cells. (Compare for example Figs. 73,
85). In the young spermatocyte (Fig. 87) the nucleus shows a

more or less conspicuous reticulum, but the nucleolus has apparently disappeared, as it usually does at this stage in other forms that have been studied. The further development of the spermatozoid corresponds very closely with that of Equisetum (see CAMPBELL — MOSSES & FERNS, 2d edit., p. 448 — BELAJAFF. Über die Cilienbildner in den Spermatogenen Zellen. Ber. der deutsch. bot. Gesells., XVI: 140, 1898). One of the blepharoplasts in the primary spermatocyte goes with each daughter cell (the definitive spermatocyte) and can be seen as a distinct rounded body near the nucleus (Fig. 87 a). In some cases what appears to be the blepharoplast lies in a depression at the periphery of the nucleus and looks very much like a nucleolus.

Before the nucleus undergoes any marked change the blepharoplast begins to elongate (Figs. 80—88) and assumes the form of a pointed, slender, strongly stained body lying close to the nucleus. This is really somewhat ribbon-shaped, and more pointed at one end than the other. It is usually somewhat curved even in its earliest stages, and the transverse section (Fig. 80 b) appears crescent shaped. The nucleus next elongates slightly and the reticulate structure becomes very conspicuous (Figs. 90—91) with large strongly stained granules which are probably composed of several more or less coherent chromosomes, as the number of these is very much less than the chromosomes in the nuclear plate of the dividing nucleus of the primary spermatocyte. The blepharoplast continues to grow, and at this stage (Figs. 91—92) is already strongly curved, and in favorable cases the young cilia can be·detected — but none of the writer's preparations showed this nearly so plainly as BALAJEFF's figures for Equisetum and Gymnogramme. There is no doubt, however, that the cilia arise in much the same way as he describes for those forms. The nucleus next becomes indented on one side and assumes a crescent shape, which elongates, becoming also more or less flattened. One end becomes narrower and sharply pointed, the other remaining thicker and rounded. The thick reticulum stains now with great intensity, and shows a tendency to coalesce, which in the final stage, results in an almost homogeneous, deeply staining mass, composed apparently of the closely coalescent chromosones. In successful preparations the nucleus stains at this stage a clear carmine red, in strong contrast to the bright violet of the blepharoplast. With the coalescence of the chromosomes the volume of the nucleus is noticeably decreased (Fig. 93).

The blepharoplast forms a spirally coiled narrow band from which the cilia can be seen to grow, following its curve, but the blepharoplast is not in close contrast with the nucleus and in transverse sections is sometimes seen quite free from it (Figs. 83, 92). The spermatocytes and the nuclei are rather smaller in *O. moluccanum* than in *O. pendulum*. In the older stages of the spermatozoid, the nucleus in the former species is decidedly more elongated and more sharply pointed at both ends (Figs. 81, 82). In this respect it more nearly resembles the spermatozoids of the true ferns, while in the larger, comparatively short nucleus, as well as in some other respects the spermatozoid of *O. pendulum* is strikingly like that of Equisetum. The number of cilia is large, but the exact number could not be determined.

Surrounding the spermatozoid and included in its coils is a considerable amount of cytoplasm, which presumably forms the central vesicle as well as the anterior coils of the free spermatozoid. It was not possible to obtain any living spermatozoids, but in a number of sections of the opened antheridium some were found in which the spermatozoids had been retained. While these were usually more or less distorted, still some were very well fixed and gave a fair idea of the structure of the free spermatozoid (Figs. 95—96). The cilia were very imperfectly preserved, in most cases, but in some of these they were plainly seen (Fig. 96). There is one very thick posterior coil mainly composed of the very large nucleus, which is much larger than that of the sperm cell shortly before it is discharged from the antheridium. The nucleus has the form of a slightly coiled thick band, tapering somewhat at both ends, but more markedly so in front. Beyond this extends a second coil apparently composed mainly of cytoplasm, but the exact origin of this is not quite clear. This second coil extends into a third much smaller one which, so far as could be made out, seems to be a flattened band along whose upper edge the blepharoplast is closely applied (Figs. 95—96). The resemblance of the spermatozoid to that of Equisetum is very striking, but the nucleus is even more shortened than in the latter. In size the spermatozoid of *O. pendulum* is probably superior to that of any other Pteridophyte. The cytoplasmic envelope and vesicle are not very clearly separated, and probably are similar to those of *O. vulgatum* or of Equisetum. In some cases seen (Fig. 96) this protoplasmic envelope completely surrounds the lower part of the spermatozoid and recalls somewhat the peculiar spermatozoid of the Cycads. Owing to their large size the spermatozoids were often sectioned, and in many sections the blepharoplast was seen free from the body of the spermatozoid, and the attachment of the cilia was very evident.

METTENIUS figures the free spermatozoids of *O. pedunculosum*, but his figures are certainly not accurate. BRUCHMANN, who has figured those of *O. vulgatum*, found that they resembled the spermatozoids of the true ferns, but were more massive, and the vesicle which envelopes the posterior coils adheres more closely to the spermatozoid than is usual in ferns. He did not, however, trace the spermatogenesis. LANG was unable to obtain the spermatozoids of *O. pendulum*, and gives no information as to their structure.

JEFFREY figures the spermatozoids of *Botrychium virginianum*, and BRUCHMANN those of *B. Lunaria*. Certain stages of the development were described by JEFFREY, but he did not see the blepharoplast nor did he study the origin of the cilia. In both species of Botrychium the spermatozoids are decidedly smaller than those of any of the species of Ophioglossum so far as could be judged from the free spermatozoids of *O. pendulum* found inside the open antheridium (Figs. 95—96); these closely resemble those of *O. vulgatum*, as figured by BRUCHMANN, but are decidedly larger.

THE ARCHEGONIUM.

Only a very small number of the young archegonia were found in *O. moluccanum*, and so no complete study of its development was possible; but as the adult archegonium of this species does not appear to differ materially from that of *O. pendulum* it is probable that its development is the same as in the latter. The account given here is based almost entirely upon a study of *O. pendulum* of which a very complete series of archegonia was secured. LANG figures accurately several stages of the archegonium of this species, and BRUCHMANN gives a series of figures illustrating the development of the archegonium in *O. vulgatum*. The latter writer failed to see the two nuclei of the neck canal cell which LANG correctly figures for *O. pendulum*. These two nuclei are invariably present in both *O. pendulum* and *O. moluccanum*, and they presumably also occur in *O. vulgatum* as they are constantly present in *Botrychium virginianum* and in all of the true ferns that have been accurately examined, as well as in Equisetum. Neither LANG nor BRUCHMANN saw the ventral canal cell, which is exceedingly difficult of demonstration. JEFFREY, however, describes this in *B. virginiamum*, and it probably is always present.

As in the case of the antheridium, the youngest archegonia may be found near the apex of the branch (Fig. 97), but may also arise at a considerable distance back of it. In general, like the antheridia, they arise in acropetal succession.

The earliest stages closely resemble the corresponding ones of the antheridium, and like the antheridium, the mother cell is sometimes broad, sometimes narrow and deep, (Figs. 98, 99) and the cover cell is correspondingly shallow or deep. Shortly after the primary cover cell is formed the inner cell divides into a central and a basal cell, as in the typical ferns. The central cell as usual gives rise to the egg-cell and the canal cells.

The next division is in the cover cell, which divides by a vertical wall (Fig. 101) and almost immediately there is a second division resulting in the four primary neck cells, which in cross section present the usual quadrant arrangement (Fig. 97). The middle cell next divides by a transverse wall into the primary neck canal cell and the central cell (Fig. 103) from which, subsequently a small ventral canal cell is cut off. The canal cell pushes up between the four primary neck cells, which presently divide by nearly horizontal walls (Fig. 104), so that there are two tiers of neck cells. One or both of these divide again, and each row of neck cells consists of three or four (Figs. 105—108). Rarely there may be five cells in one or more of the rows.

The neck canal cell is very conspicuous, its base being broad and the upper part narrower and extended to the uppermost neck cells. The large and conspicuous nucleus soon divides into two, but as a rule there is no division wall formed. In one case, however, (Fig. 107) there were two distinct neck canal cells. Sometimes both of the nuclei remain in the broad basal part of the cell, and sometimes one is at the base and one nearer the apex. This arrangement seems to depend upon the direction in which the nuclear division takes place.

The basal cell divides by a vertical wall at about the same time that the primary canal cell is cut off from the central cell. The basal cell subsequently undergoes further divisions, but its limits are readily distinguishable up to the time that the archegonium is mature (Figs. 106, 109).

In its earlier stages the archegonium of *O. pendulum* bears a striking resemblance to that of the Marattiaceae, which the mature archegonium more closely resembles than it does that of Botrychium. Compared with *O. vulgatum*, the neck is decidedly shorter, and this difference is still more marked when compared with Botrychium, especially *Botrychium virginianum*. Even when mature, the neck projects but little above the surface of the prothallium, although there is an elongation of the cells at the time of dehiscence (Figs. 108, 109).

The ventral canal cell is extremely difficult to demonstrate, and one might be inclined to doubt whether it is formed at all, in some cases, were it not that it is always present in all other Archegoniates that have been critically examined. It is more likely that its absence in most of the archegonia is due to the fact that it is formed very late, and is extremely inconspicuous. The same apparent absence of a ventral canal cell in the Cycads and some Conifers has been shown, on more critical study of the material, to be due to the small size of the ventral nucleus and its very evanescent character. In one case (Fig. 110) there seemed no doubt about the presence of this cell, and in nearly all the archegonia examined just before they opened there was present a vesicular body above the egg, and this was probably the ventral canal cell much distended with fluid preparatory to the opening of the archegonium. A small nucleus, or what looked like one, could be seen in a few cases, but it must be said that its nuclear nature was not above suspicion (Figs. 103, 111).

Just before the archegonium is ready to open, the egg-cell, which, up to this time, is compressed above by the basal wall of the neck canal cell, becomes rounded and pushes up the base of the canal cell, which becomes convex upward. It is about this period that the ventral canal cell is cut off. It appears (Fig. 110) as a very narrow cell in which the nucleus can be only imperfectly made out, as it seems to be extremely compressed and is very much smaller than the nucleus of the egg. Unfortunately no cases were found showing the mitosis in the central cell, but there seemed no reason to doubt that this narrow cell is really the ventral canal cell. Very soon this cell becomes much enlarged, and appears almost transparent, owing to its scanty contents (Fig. 108).

The neck canal cell does not show the complete disorganisation which is common, but retains its form up to time the archegonium opens. With the opening of the neck there is some elongation of the outer neck cells, but there is decidedly less projection about the surface of the prothallium than is the case in *O. vulgatum*. The nucleus of the egg-cell is large, but it does not always stain readily except for the nucleoli, and it may be that the same resistence to stains is the reason why the sister nucleus in the ventral canal-cell is so difficult to see.

In three instances spermatozoids were seen in the neck and venter of the open archegonium, and twice a spermatozoid was seen in the nucleus of the egg, but there were no other stages obtained, so that the details of the nuclear fusion could not be followed. It probably, however, is much the same as that described by Shaw for Onoclea. (The Fertilization of Onoclea, Ann. of Bot., XII: 261—285, 1898). In the mature egg-cell the nuclear reticulum is often decidedly contracted, but whether this is normal or the result of reagents can not be said.

THE EMBRYO.

A special effort was made to obtain embryos, as both LANG and BRUCHMANN were unable to procure the earlier stages of the development of the embryo. Indeed, LANG figures but a single somewhat advanced stage in O. pendulum. BRUCHMANN succeeded in obtaining two-celled stages, and a single more advanced embryo of O. vulgatum, and he also describes and figures several stages of the young sporophyte. METTENIUS's figures of the embryo of O. pedunculosum are not satisfactory, but he shows correctly sections of the young sporophyte after it has broken through the prothallium.

In O. moluccanum where most of the prothallia develop sporophytes, the small number of young prothallia that was available made it impossible to obtain a series of young embryos. A single one of two cells (Fig. 116) and one older embryo were all that could be found. The young sporophytes, however, were found in a sufficiently early stage of development to make clear some very important points bearing on the structure of the young sporophyte. In this species the further growth of the gametophyte is stopped by the development of the sporophyte, and only rarely is more than one sporophyte formed.

In O. pendulum a fairly complete series of embryos was obtained, and the development was followed quite satisfactorily.

From a study of these two species it is evident that the history of the young sporophyte is very different from that of any other Pteridophyte, and in both species the definitive sporophyte always arises secondarily as a bud upon the root in the same way that there are so commonly formed adventitious buds upon the roots of the adult sporophyte. BRUCHMANN notes in *O. vulgatum* the very precocious development of the primary root and the late appearance of the stem apex and first leaf; but in this species the shoot apex seems to be derived directly from the epibasal half of the embryo, as it is in most Pteridophytes.

The youngest embryo found by the writer in *O. moluccanum* (Fig. 116) had two cells. In this the basal wall was nearly transverse, as it usually is in the eusporangiate ferns.

In *O. pendulum* where the development of the embryo seems to offer no check to the further growth of the prothallium, the position of the archegonium is very various, and it is impossible to see from the section what the position was in the living state, as the branches of the gametophyte extend in all directions and archegonia may be formed at any point upon their surface. To judge from the youngest stages of the embryo that were met with (Figs. 118, 119) the basal wall in this species is not necessarily transverse to the axis of the archegonium. In both of these cases it was oblique, but more nearly longitudinal than transverse. It is very likely, however, that it may be horizontal, or approximately so. In the four-celled embryo shown in Fig. 118, the quadrant walls were at right angles to each other, and this was also the case in the five-celled embryo shown in Fig. 119.

Somewhat older embryos (Figs. 117, 120) show that there is a pretty regular octant formation, and BRUCHMANN states that this is also the case in *O. vulgatum*. BRUCHMANN and JEFFREY found a similar state of things in Botrychium.

While in all typical ferns and in Botrychium all of the organs of the young plant can be traced to certain regions of the young embryo, in *O. pendulum* only a single one of the definitive organs so arises, the root, and this becomes differentiated at a very early period. One of the octants next the archegonium (Fig. 117) becomes at once the apical cell of the young root. This cell is very soon recognizable by its size and shape, and quickly begins its regular segmentation. The primary cap-cell is soon cut off (Fig. 120) and from this time on the young root is very conspicuous. Figures 121—123 show three transverse sections of an embryo about the same age as that shown in Figure 120. The octant divisions are very clearly marked here, and in section c, which is the uppermost of the three, the large triangular apical cell of the primary root is very evident.

Two types of the older embryo were seen. One of these is nearly globular in form (Figs. 124—125) the other elongated (Figs. 126, 129). The former looks as if it originated from an embryo in which the basal wall was transverse to the axis of the archegonium; in the other it was probably more or less vertical. It is probable that in the former instance the root initial is one of the epibasal octants while the whole of the hypobasal portion forms the large foot. In the second type it is difficult to say which half should be considered epibasal, and which hypobasal, but as in the other case one-half may be considered to be root, the other half foot, the growth of both being nearly in a plane at right angles to that of the archegonium axis. Figure 125 is a nearly median section of an embryo of the first type, and it is not unlike JEFFREY's Figure 48 of the embryo of *Botrychium virginianum*. The whole lower portion, (hypobasal half), forms the very conspicuous foot, while from the epibasal region the root is developing and already the rudiment of the second root (r^2) is visible. Whether the latter arises directly from the primary root or whether it may arise independently from the second epibasal quadrant is not quite certain. At this stage the central vascular bundle of the primary root is clearly evident, but no tracheary tissue is yet visible. The cells of the epibasal part of the embryo are evidently much more active, having abundant protoplasm and conspicuous nuclei. The cells of the foot are larger and much more transparent.

The second type of embryo (Figs. 126, 129) resembles closely a certain stage of the embryo of *O. vulgatum* (BRUCHMANN, Fig. 58) where, as BRUCHMANN says, the embryo is "all root". He considers that the root and foot are both of hypobasal origin, but he bases this rather on a comparison with the true ferns than upon actual study of embryos, as he was unable to obtain embryos sufficiently young to demonstrate this, and all trace of the original divisions disappears before any sign of the stem and leaf is evident. It may be well questioned whether, as in Botrychium and *O. pendulum* the foot does not take up the whole hypobasal region. It is not impossible that the position of the basal wall may also vary in *O. vulgatum*. From a comparison with the embryo of *O. pendulum* the writer is inclined to assign more of the embryo of *O. vulgatum* to the foot region than is done by BRUCHMANN.

In *O. vulgatum*, however, there is finally a differentiation of the stem apex from the epibasal region, as in Botrychium and the true ferns, while, as we shall see, in *O. pendulum* the embryo develops simply the primary root, from which (or possibly independently, from the sister quadrant) the second root is developed, and there is no trace either of stem or leaf. These first appear upon a bud which develops endogenously from the older root.

While in *O. moluccanum* the prothallium probably only lives for a single season and the formation of the sporophyte stops its further development, in *O. pendulum*, where embryos are much less frequently found, the large gametophyte continues its growth apparently unchecked by the development of the attached sporophyte, which retains its connection for a very long time, as in *O. vulgatum* and *Botrychium virginianum*.

The embryo reaches a very large size before it breaks through the prothallium. The primary root then pushes through, as a conical point (Fig. 40). The second root remains short for a time. There seems to be a good deal of difference as to the period of the appearance of the latter. In the globular type of embryo the rudiment of the second root is very early apparent (Fig. 125) and it looks as if it were formed quite independently of the primary root. In some cases (Fig. 41) the primary root may attain a length of several centimeters, and may even begin to form secondary roots before the second root emerges. In other cases (Fig. 42) the two roots grow in opposite directions and seem to be equally massive.

In searching for young germ plants, no very small ones were seen — the smallest leaves being some 20 centimeters or more in length, and these were invariably connected with a root bud and in no cases with the prothallium directly. Not realizing that these were the young sporophytes growing as buds upon the root of the embryo, no effort was made at the time to trace their connection with the latter, and unfortunately it therefore cannot be stated just when they make their appearance. The primary root, although attaining a length of 10 centimeters or more, in no cases showed any signs of the leaf-bearing bud in any specimens that were collected. Rootlets were observed in some instances (Fig. 41) and it is not impossible that there may be an extensive development of a root-system before the first leafy bud is formed. This is quite in harmony with the large development of the roots in *O. vulgatum*, where BRUCHMANN believes that it may be eight or ten years before the first foliage leaf appears above the ground. In *O. vulgatum*, however, this leaf arises from the original stem apex derived directly from the embryo and not from an adventitious bud.

The terrestrial species of Ophioglossum collected at Buitenzorg (and this was also the case with the one collected at Hakgala) differ very much from *O. pendulum* in the character of the young sporophyte, but as already has been stated, the early stages of the embryo could not be followed. The type of the sporophyte is closely like that of *O. pedunculosum* described by METTENIUS, and so close is the resemblance that it would seem to confirm the close relationship of this species and possibly its identity with some of the forms associated under the name *O. moluccanum*, by RACIBORSKI. There was, however, no way of certainly identifying the young plants, as all the species grow together so that it is by no means certain that all the embryos or young sporophytes described, really belong to the same species. However, they all agree very closely, and it is doubtful whether there is any great difference among them.

O. moluccanum and the forms associated with it differ strikingly from both *O. vulgatum* and *O. pendulum*. As METTENIUS correctly showed in *O. pedunculosum*, the first organ to be developed is a leaf (cotyledon) which soon pierces the earth and appears as a green foliage leaf above its surface. This primary leaf is continued directly into the primary root, (Fig. 132) but no stem apex is developed nor is any sheath formed about the leaf base in the young sporophyte, which consists simply of leaf and root. The latter often penetrates for some distance into the prothallial tissue before it emerges so that the central portion of the young sporophyte is surrounded by a sheath formed by the prothallial tissue (Fig. 135). A longitudinal section of the sporophyte (Fig. 135) shows that the tissues of the leaf are continued directly into those of the primary root. A single axial vascular bundle traverses the whole of the young sporophyte without interruption, and there is no evident boundary between the tissues of the leaf base and those of the root. The central region of the embryo is somewhat broader and its outer cells slightly enlarged, but no clearly marked foot can at this time be recognized. The strictly bipolar character of the young sporophyte and the way in which it perforates the gametophyte resemble most nearly corresponding stages of Equisetum and the Marattiaceae. LYON's recent note on *Botrychium obliquum* is interesting in this connection, as there is a similar bipolar arrangement of leaf and root in that species. The sporophyte in the latter also perforates the prothallium much as is the case in the Marattiaceae, and there is no clear development of a foot. LYON, however, states that in this species there is a suspensor, and figures this in the young sporophyte. If this should prove to be a constant character of *B. obliquum*, it would be a very great departure from the condition found in all other members of the family. As Mettenius correctly pointed out, the definitive sporophyte arises as an adventitious bud from the primary root, either close to the leaf base, or more commonly at some distance from it (Fig. 145). In one case observed by the writer two independent sporophytes were found growing from the same prothallium, (Fig. 28) but this is unusual, and most of the cases where two sporophytes appear to be present one of these can be shown to be the secondary sporophyte attached to the primary root of the first formed one.

While in *O. vulgatum* the sporophyte vegetates under ground for several years, in *O. moluccanum* there is every reason to believe that there is only a brief interval between the first formation of the leaf and its appearance above ground. The small size and the character of the gametophyte, as well as the rapid germination of the spores and the rapid growth natural to a tropical climate, indicate that the gametophyte is annual, and that it dies as soon as the young sporophyte is established.

In one case the rudiment of the bud was found close to the apex of the primary root (Fig. 137 *k*), but usually it is found at an intermediate point, but well removed from the base. In the younger stages met with, the bud was already multicellular, its cells distinguished from those of surrounding tissues, by staining more strongly and showing evidences of active growth. At a very early period (Fig. 147) the stem apex is indicated by the presence of a small group of large cells, one of which is probably the single apical cell; but in no cases observed did this show the tetrahedral form which has been found in other species of *Ophioglossum*. This cell, in longitudinal section, is somewhat wedge-shaped, broadly truncate at the base instead of pointed, as in other species of *Ophioglossum* that have been studied. Bruchmann does not specifically state that the apical cell of the stem in *O. vulgatum* is tetrahedral, but his figures indicate this, and in the adult sporophyte of *O. pendulum* the writer has described and figured such a cell (Mosses and Ferns, 2d edit., Fig. 134).

The shoot apex lies in a narrow depression between the base of the leaf and a narrow ridge which extends around it on the side opposite the leaf base. This latter structure is the beginning of the conical sheath characteristic of the shoot apex of the older sporophyte. In the only transverse section of the young shoot apex that was obtained the apical cell was triangular, as in the other species that have been examined (Fig. 148.*x*).

The leaf forms a conical body with a definite apical cell of tetrahedral form. The apex of the first leaf and stem of the bud are formed quite independently of each other, and in the older stages, when the young vascular bundles belonging to each are developed, they very often are entirely distinct, connecting with the vascular bundle of the root from which the bud arises at points some distance apart (Fig. 149). Indeed this is sometimes so marked that there is an appearance of two distinct buds side by side, one of which forms the leaf and the other the stem rudiment.

The leaf rapidly elongates and soon breaks through the overlying root tissues (Fig. 145). A longitudinal section of a bud at this period shows the stem apex at the bottom of a cup-shaped depression, with the apical cell conspicuous, as well as its youngest segments. The beginning of the vascular strands of leaf and stem can be seen starting from tracheids which are now visible in the vascular cylinder of the root from which the bud is developed.

The first root of the bud itself does not appear until a later period, and it is formed within the stem rudiment. Possibly as in other cases, the apical cell of the root is derived from an endodermal cell of the stem bundle. In the earliest stage that was encountered, however, the root was already established, and its exact origin could not be determined. There is soon evident a central strand connecting wirh the young vascular cylinder of the stem. By this time also the central vascular strand of the leaf is clearly evident, and the apical cell of the leaf is readily made out. It is, however, not until a much later stage that the tracheary tissue is formed.

The root of the young bud does not emerge until the leaf is nearly complete. From this time on the further growth is due to the activity of the stem apex, from which the new leaves and roots are presumably developed in the same way as in the other species that have been studied. How long it is before fertile leaves are developed was not ascertained, but in the rapidly growing species of a tropical climate it is likely that this takes place before long. The occurrence of very small fertile individuals (Fig. 154) points to this.

ANATOMY OF THE YOUNG SPOROPHYTE.

In *O. pendulum* the young primary root soon breaks through the prothallium and rapidly elongates, but owing to its brittleness, it is easily broken off, and it is impossible to state here just how far it develops before the bud is formed upon it. The development of the second root varies much. The first root sometimes reaches a length of three or four centimeters before the second root can be seen at all. The growth of roots is in all respects similar to that of the later ones. There is a large tetrahedral apical cell whose divisions are quite regular, and there is soon visible the axial vascular bundle which extends for some distance into the foot, where it ends blindly. The vascular bundle of the second root joins the first at the junction of bundle of the latter with that of the foot (Fig. 127).

The first tracheary tissue appears at the point of junction — short, somewhat irregular pointed tracheids with reticulate thickenings. From this point the development of the tracheary tissue proceeds toward the apex of the roots. As in the later roots, the bundle is diarch, as is plainly seen from cross sections (Fig. 144). The endodermis is very clearly defined, and the characteristic radial markings are extraordinarily clear, especially in sections treated with a double stain of safranine and gentian violet. The tracheary tissue is also beautifully differentiated by this stain. The bundle is slightly elliptical in form, and the protoxylem elements appear at the foci of the elliptical section. The first appearance of the tracheary tissue is at some distance back of the apex, and the development appears to go on rather slowly. In the oldest part of the roots examined, the two xylem masses were unequal in size, the largest showing about half a dozen tracheids in cross section, the other, two or three. Whether the two protoxylems are ultimately joined by intermediate tracheal tissue so as to form a continuous plate, as in the roots of the adult plant, cannot now be stated, but in no cases examined was this the case, and it is probable that in the primary root the two xylem masses remain permanently separated. The cells of the foot, as usual, are more or less papillate where they are in contact with the tissue of the gametophyte. They early become infected with the endophyte, which probably makes its entrance from the prothallial tissue, and not from the outside. This point, however, is not perfectly clear. The infected area follows the growth of the young root, but leaves the apical tissues free.

In *O. moluccanum* the leaf is the first part of the young sporophyte to develop. In the one large embryo obtained the leaf formed a conical body, merging into a nearly globular basal portion, partly foot, partly the beginning of the root, whose apical cell was already manifest. The leaf shows a definite apical cell, triangular in section, and exhibiting regular segmentation. The inner cells of the segments form the axial strand of tissue which is continued through the embryo into the root. The limits of the two primary organs are quite indistinguishable. The central region which remains surrounded by the prothallial tissue is somewhat larger in diameter and the whole of this functions as a foot, although it is composed in part of tissue belonging to the root and leaf. The conical young leaf elongates rapidly after it has ruptured the calyptra, and its apex begins to widen out, but still shows a single apical cell (Fig. 131). In the case figured, the vascular cylinder (plerome) becomes widened abruptly a short distance below the apex, probably primarily due to the rapid widening of the young lamina of the leaf in which the reticulately arranged vascular bundles are soon clearly differentiated.

The fully developed cotyledon in what may be considered the typical form of·O. moluccanum (Fig. 133) is more or less lanceolate in outline. There is a central vein from which veins branch on either side, connecting with the central vein by anastomosing branches so as to enclose elongated meshes. In the form with broader leaves, (Fig. 32) probably another species, the mid-vein is more obscure and the areoles are broader and more numerous.

As already indicated, the vascular strand of the young sporophyte is continuous, and sections at different points show essentially the same structure. The petiole of the cotyledon (Fig. 142) which is traversed by two large lacunae shows the axial bundle to be markedly collateral in structure. The xylem consists of a group of about half a dozen tracheids at the inner limit of the bundle whose endodermis is not clearly visible. As the section of the bundle is made in the mid-region of the sporophyte (Fig. 141) the only difference noted is a slightly greater development of the tracheary tissue. The section of the root presents almost exactly the same appearance as that of the leaf. Whether we should call the root-bundle monarch or collateral is merely a question of terms. In the mid-region the endodermis can be clearly made out, and it is seen that the xylem is separated from it by a single layer of pericambium cells.

If the gametophyte of Ophioglossum is compared with that of the other genera of the family it is found to be most like that of Helminthostachys, with which it agrees in its radial structure, while the gametophyte of Botrychium is dorsi-ventral. The marked radial character of the prothallium of all the species of Ophioglossum is noteworthy, and it is probably to be attributed to the absence of light, although this does not seem to apply to Botrychium, which in the absence of light develops a dorsi-ventral prothallium. Some recent experiments of PEIRCE (Studies of Irritability in Plants, Ann. of Bot., LXXX : 449, 1906) upon Anthoceros and certain liverworts may be interesting in this connection. While in *Fimbriaria californica* and the prothallium of *Gymnogramme triangularis* equal exposure to light on a klinostat could not destroy the tendency to bilateral development, in Anthoceros it was quite annhilated by this equal illumination. BRUCHMANN states that the prothallium of *O. vulgatum* will develop chlorophyll under the influence of light, but will not become flattened. The writer has kept prothallia of *O. pendulum* exposed to the light for more than two months without any evidence of chlorophyll being developed, nor is there any change in the form, although the growth continues slowly, and apparently in a perfectly healthy way.

Assuming that *O. moluccanum* would behave much as *O. pedunculosum*, which it otherwise so closely resembles, we may assume that it represents the most primitive of the three types — *O. moluccanum*, *O. vulgatum* and *O. pendulum*. The occasional slight development of chlorophyll in the germinating spores and the power to develop chlorophyll later under exposure to light point to this type being nearest the green gametophyte from which presumably these colorless saprophytic forms have arisen.

The rapidity of spore germination and the delicacy and small size of the older gametophyte, as we have already pointed out, indicates that in *O. moluccanum* the gametophyte is an annual structure. This is probably also the case with Helminthostachys. Many prothallia of the latter, with the young sporophyte attached, were collected by the writer in Ceylon, but all were practically of the same age. They were growing in a forest which was periodically submerged, and it looked as if in this plant, as in *O. moluccanum*, complete submersion in water was a necessary condition for germination. The hot, humid climate where both forms flourish would naturally induce a rapid growth, and it is hardly likely that the small prothallium, developing regularly its single sporophyte, would require more than one season for its growth. It is possible that the more plastic character of Ophioglossum with reference to the influence of light as compared with Botrychium may be an indication of the more primitive character of the genus. Thus in PEIRCE's experiment Fimbriaria and Gymnogramme are undoubtedly more specialized types than Anthoceros which was much more plastic than the former. This view would also harmonize with the relative behavior of *O. moluccanum* and *O. pendulum* with respect to the development of chlorophyll in response to exposure to light. The saprophytic habit becomes far more marked in *O. pendulum*, where the gametophyte reaches a very great size and develops unlimited power of multiplication. This may be assumed perhaps to be connected with its epiphytic habit.

As has been urged by the writer before (MOSSES & FERNS, 2d edit., p. 278) the similarity of the sexual organs in *Ophioglossum* and the Marattiaceae is very great, and there are also strong points of resemblance to Equisetum, which we are inclined to believe belongs to the same great series as the eusporangiate ferns. The form of both archegonium and antheridium is strikingly similar, and the very large spermatozoids of Ophioglossum are more like those of Equisetum than like those of any true fern. Presumably the ancestral type from which Ophioglossum came, had a large green prothallium not so very different from that of the Marattiaceae or, possibly may have been a branching green gametophyte like that found in Anthoceros or Equisetum. There might also be considered in this connection the chlorophylless prothallium of Isoetes, whose archegonium and embryo have a certain resemblance to those of the Ophioglossaceae, and whose spermatozoids are also multiciliate.

Three types of embryo may be recognized in Ophioglossum represented respectively by *O. moluccanum, O. vulgatum* and *O. pendulum*. If, as seems not unlikely *O. moluccanum* is the most primitive of the three, some interesting points arise as to the significance of the peculiarities exhibited by the embryo which shows only two organs, aside from the very poorly defined foot, viz., the cotyledon and primary root; and these grow in almost exactly opposite directions without any clear line of demarcation between them. The writer (MOSSES and FERNS, 2d edit., p. 600) has ventured to draw a comparision between the sporophyte of Ophioglossum and that of Anthoceros, assuming that the former has arisen from some type not unlike Anthoceros, by the development of a root from the base of the sporogonium and of a special foliar organ from the basal meristem of such a sporogonium. This view was strengthened by the discovery of the remarkable *O. simplex* (see BOWER, Ann. of Bot., 205, 1904) which nearly fulfilled the hypothetical form suggested by the writer. The embryo of *O. moluccanum* comes still nearer this hypothetical form, as it consists only of leaf and root and no stem apex is developed from it, its growth being of limited duration. In this case the definitive sporophyte is a secondary structure developed as a bud upon the primary root.

In *O. vulgatum*, however, the definitive stem apex, although of very late origin, is nevertheless a product of the original embryonic tissue, although the first foliage leaf is of much later origin. In *O. pendulum* the formation of the leafy sporophyte is secondary, as in *O. moluccanum*, but neither stem apex nor leaf is produced from the embryo itself.

If, as the writer believes, Ophioglossum represents the most primitive type of the fern series of Pteridophytes, it is quite conceivable that in *O. moluccanum* and its allies the embryo represents the condition existing in the ancestral type from which these have sprung. On the supposition that the leafy sporophyte is derived from a large bryophytic sporogonium resembling that of Anthoceros, there must have been a stage when the sporophyte consisted of two parts only, the upper sporogenous portion, which developed into a sporophyll, as represented in Ophioglossum, and the root. Of course it is quite possible that the peculiar origin of the definitive sporophyte in *O. moluccanum* and *O. pedunculosum* it secondary, but this is by no means necessarily the case. However, it seems highly probable that the extraordinary development of the roots in *O. pendulum* and *O. vulgatum* and the protracted subterranean life in these species, is a secondary phenomenon associated with the pronounced saprophytic life of the gametophyte.

Admitting that *O. moluccanum* represents the most primitive type of the group, we should assume that from this was developed in one direction the type of *O. pendulum*, in which the development of roots and the long subterranean life are intensified by its marked saprophytic habit, but in which the final development of the definitive sporophyte is essentially the same as in *O. moluccanum*.

In another direction the formation of the stem apex is referable to the embryo itself, and the definitive sporophyte is the direct product of the embryo. This condition becomes more strongly marked in Botrychium and Helminthostachys, between which and *O. moluccanum*, *O. vulgatum* may be said to form an intermediate stage.

Among the other Pteridophytes there are two groups which show some points of resemblance to the type of embryo found in Ophioglossum. In both Equisetum and the Marattiaceae there is the same bipolar arrangement of the primary organs. In the Marattiaceae the cotyledon grows upward through the prothallial tissues and the root downward, the young embryo in section presenting an appearance not very different from that found in *O. moluccanum* except that the stem apex is present. The same is true of *Botrychium obliquum*.

The resemblance in Equisetum is not so obvious as naturally the relation, if it exists, is far more remote. However, it is conceivable that from the same original type as that from which Ophioglossum came, there may have developed one in which the epibasal region formed a conical body with its apical cell, and developed into a single spore-bearing structure — the leaf as we have it in Ophioglossum. In another direction the same rudiment formed a stem apex, such as occurs in Equisetum. It is interesting to note that in Equisetum, as in *O. moluccanum* and *O. pendulum*, the definitive axis of the adult sporophyte is formed secondarily, the primary shoot derived from the embryo having only a limited growth. While probably only an analogy, it is worth considering, as showing a tendency at least to a similar course of development in the sporophytes of the two genera.

THE SIGNIFICANCE OF THE ENDOPHYTE.

There has been some question as to the exact role of the endophyte in the economy of the plant. That it is essential to the development of the prothallium is shown by the history of the germination of the spores. Where the connection with the fungus is established, the growth is accelerated, and the further development of the gametophyte is made possible, while in no cases is it able to develop without this association. In the latter case the young gametophyte perishes after the reserve food in the spore is exhausted.

It is probable that the principal role of the fungus is in the assimilation of the organic constituents from the humus. In a subterranean chlorophylless gametophyte photo-synthesis is of course out of the question, and the carbon compounds must be obtained from the organic matter in the humus. It is probably in this connection that the symbiotic activity of the fungus comes into play. Just how this is accomplished must be determined by experiment.

It is not probable that the fungus plays any important part in the actual absorption of food elements from the soil. It is rather in the metabolic processes within the thallus that the fungus is especially useful. BRUCHMANN (Über das Prothallium und die Sporenpflanze von Botrychium Lunaria, Flora 96 : 211, 1906) thinks that the great amount of oil developed by the endophyte is probably of use as a protection against dessication to which the prothallium may be exposed. The writer found that the prothallia of *O. pendulum* could be quite dried up for a short period without being killed, but as this is also true of certain green fern prothallia, e. g., *Gymnogramme triangularis*, where there is no large amount of oil developed, it is not likely that this is a prominent function of the endophyte.

The infection of the young sporophyte takes place in both *O. moluccanum* and *O. pendulum* at an early period, and at the time the young sporophyte breaks through the prothallial tissue the endophyte is well established. It first appears in the foot, and from there follows the development of the root. There is no difference in appearance between the endophyte in the gametophyte and that in the root of the sporophyte; although the actual passage of the fungus from the prothallial tissue into the young sporophyte was not detected, there seemes little question that the infection of the sporophyte is mainly from the prothallial tissue, and not from the mycorhiza outside, as BRUCHMANN thinks is the case in *O. vulgatum*.

The presence of an endophytic fungus is not confined to a chlorophylless gametophyte. They have also been observed in a large number of liverworts (HUMPHREY — The Development of *Fossombronia longiseta*, Ann. of Bot. XX : 87, 1906). In looking over some old preparations of Osmunda the writer found a prothallium of *O. cinnamomea* in which there was an abundant endophyte closely resembling that found in the Ophioglossaceae. Whether this is a common occurrence in Osmunda remains to be seen. In the green gametophyte it may be assumed that the symbiotic nature of the fungus is more or less questionable, but it is important to find that such an endophyte may exist in a green prothallium, as this would help to explain its presence in the saprophytic gametophyte of Ophioglossum. It will be interesting to discover whether or not such endophytic fungi also occur in any Marattiaceae or Gleicheniaceae.

THE SPECIES OF OPHIOGLOSSUM IN JAVA.

RACIBORSKI (Die Pteridophyten der Flora von Buitenzorg, 1898) records only two species of Ophioglossum in Java — *O. moluc-canum* SCHLECT. and *O. pendulum* L. Later (Die Farne von Tegal, Natuurkundig Tijdschrift, LIX) he calls attention to some of the variations in the former, but does not propose any new species.

It is clear that there are at least three species which have been confused under the name *O. moluccanum.* Specimens of these were sent by the writer to Mrs. E. G. Britton of the New York botanical garden, who has carefully studied the American species of genus, and she submitted them also to Professor L. M. Underwood. Both agreed that there were three distinct species. What seems to be the typical *O. moluccanum* is shown in Fig. 153. It is a plant of moderate size, with usually a lanceolate sterile leaf segment, and long stalked spike with about 30 sporangia. Forms of apparently the same species vary much in size, and sometimes have a leaf more nearly cordate in form. The spores in this species (Fig. 155) are of moderate size, with a conspicuously reticulate exospore. This was the form which germinated most readily.

A second species is about the same size or a little larger, with a markedly cordate leaf, and much larger spores (Fig. 157). The latter have a finely reticulate exospore and much less granular contents than in the typical *O. moluccanum.* A very marked peculiarity of the spores of this species is the fact that they almost always have two nuclei, and may even be divided into two cells, a peculiarity which, so far as the writer is aware, is not known in any other homosporous Pteridophyte. None of these spores could be made to germinate.

The third species was smaller than the others, with short and broad — sometimes almost kidney-shaped — sterile segments of the leaf and very small finely reticulate spores (Fig. 139). Besides these three associated species, there also occurs in the neighborhood of Buitenzorg the interesting *O. intermedium* Hooker collected first near Buitenzorg by Dr. J. J. Smith. This has hitherto been known only from Borneo, and the original locality has been lost. It has been supposed to be a variety of *O. pendulum* (Bitter, Ophioglossaceae in Engler & Prantl, Die natürlichen Pflanzenfamilien, 1 Th. abt. IV: 469) but there is no question that it represents a very distinct species, perhaps nearer to the peculiar *O. simplex* RIDLEY than to *O. pendulum*.

At Tjibodas, a terrestrial species of Ophioglossum was very abundant, but all attempts to grow the spores were unsuccessful, nor could any prothallia be procured, although repeated search was made for these. This species belongs to the *reticulatum* group, and closely resembles the species collected in Ceylon, and may be the same. RACIBORSKI does not seem to have collected this, as he makes no reference to any species from Tjibodas except *O. pendulum*.

It is evident that the terrestrial species of Ophioglossum of the Indo-Malayan region are very much in need of a careful revision.

SUMMARY.

The most important points brought out in the foregoing paper may be briefly summarized as follows:

1. The spores of *O. moluccanum* germinated freely and promptly, but did not proceed beyond a four-celled stage, owing, apparently, to failure to become associated with the mycorhizal fungus. Germination in *O. pendulum* was slower, but in a number of cases the association with the fungus was established, and growth continued. Prothallia of twelve to thirteen cells were obtained in this species.

2. No trace of chlorophyll was found in *O. pendulum*, but in *O. moluccanum* some of the young prothallia developed a few chloroplasts.

3. Adult prothallia were found in *O. moluccanum* and *O. pendulum*. Also in an undetermined species from Hakgala, Ceylon.

4. The gametophyte of all the species is subterranean and normally destitute of chlorophyll, and radial in structure as described by METTENIUS, BRUCHMANN and LANG. It is very large in *O. pendulum*, and apparently capable of unlimited reproduction by means of detached buds. In *O. moluccanum* it is short lived, probably living only for a single season.

5. The antheridium of all the forms examined agrees in its development with the description given by LANG and BRUCHMANN.

The spermatozoids are very large and agree closely in their development with those of Equisetum.

6. The archegonium most nearly resembles that of the Marattiaceae. Two neck canal cells may be present, and there is always a division of the canal cell nucleus. A ventral canal cell was demonstrated in *O. pendulum.*

7. The basal wall of the embryo is probably transverse in most cases, but in *O. pendulum* it often varies a good deal in position, probably due to the very variable position of the archegonium. There is also a good deal of difference in the degree of development of the foot, which is derived apparently from the whole of the hypobasal half of the young embryo.

8. There are three types of embryo in the Ophioglossum, viz., the types of *O. moluccanum, O. vulgatum* and *O. pendulum.* In the first, leaf and root only are developed. In the second, root and stem, with a late development of the foliage leaf. In the third, roots only.

9. The definitive sporophyte in both *O. moluccanum* and *O. pendulum* is formed as an adventitious bud upon the root of the embryo sporophyte.

10. In *O. moluccanum* the tissues of the cotyledon and primary root are continuous, and the structure of the axial vascular bundle is essentially the same throughout, — collateral in the leaf, monarch in the root. The primary root of *O. pendulum* is diarch, like the later roots.

11. The type of embryo in *O. moluccanum* is probably the most primitive, and has its nearest analogy in that of the Marattiaceae and Equisetum. As in these its growth is bipolar and it perforates the gametophyte in much the same way.

12. The nearest affinity of the Ophioglossum is probably with the Marattiaceae, but it is probable that there is also a remote affinity with the Equisetineae.

13. The presence of an endophytic fungus is universal in the Ophioglossaceae, and there is no difference between the form occurring in the gametophyte and in the sporophyte. In the two species under consideration there is evidence that the

infection of the sporophyte is mainly due to the endophyte within the prothallium.

14. Under the name, *O. moluccanum* SCHLECT., it is evident that at least three distinct species have been included. *O. intermedium* HOOKER must he considered as a good species.

In conclusion the writer wishes to express to Professor TREUB and his colleagues at the gardens in Buitenzorg, his great appreciation of the many kindnesses shown him during his stay in Java. These alone have made possible the collection and study of the materials upon which this paper is based.

EXPLANATION OF FIGURES.

PLATE IX.

All figures X 500.

Fig. 1. Two spores of *Ophioglossum moluccanum* showing the range in size.

Fig. 2. Two-celled stage of *O. moluccanum*.

Fig. 3. First stage of germination of a spore perhaps belonging to another species.

Figs. 4, 5. Two older stages of *O. moluccanum*. Fig. 4 shows two chloroplasts; sp. spore-membrane.

Fig. 6. A four-celled prothallium of *O. moluccanum*, seen in transverse optical section.

Fig. 7. Two views of a similar stage.

Fig. 8. Two transverse optical sections of a four-celled prothallium.

Fig. 9. Three-celled prothallium of *O. intermedium*.

Figs. 10, 11. Two germinating spores of *O. pendulum*.

Figs. 12—17. Older prothallia of *O. pendulum*, showing the infection by the mycorhiza, m. Fig. 15 is a surface view of 14, and 16 a similar view of 17.

PLATE X.

Fig. 18. Two views of a young prothallium of 13 cells, of *O pendulum*, m. mycorhiza; x, apical cell (?) x 500.

Fig. 19. Three transverse (optical) sections of a similar prothallium; x, apical cell (?).

Fig. 20. The same prothallium as in Fig. 19, seen from the side.

Fig. 21. Adult gametophyte of *O. moluccanum* t, basal tuber; ♂, antheridia: x10.

Fig. 22. Prothallium, pr. of the same species with young sporophyte; l, cotyledon, r, root; x5.

Fig. 23. Prothallium of probably another species, x 3. A bud (k) is visible at the base of the first root of the young sporophyte.

Fig. 24. Another prothallium of probably the same form.

Figs. 25, 26. Two prothallia of *O. moluccanum*, with young sporophytes attached, x5.

Fig. 27. Prothallium of *O. moluccannm*, with sporophyte attached; the leaf (l²) of the definitive sporophyte is seen arising from the primary root, r'. x5.

Fig. 28. Prothallium of *O. moluccanum*, with two independent sporophytes, x3

Fig. 29. Part of a prothallium of *O. moluccanum*, with attached sporophyte showing fully developed cotyledon l, x3.

Figs. 30, 31. Two prothallia of *O. sp.?* from Hakgala, Ceylon, x5.

Fig. 32. Prothallium and young sporophyte of *O. moluccanum* (?); broad leaved form, Buitenzorg, x3.

192

PLATE XI.

Figs. 23, 43, 44, *O. moluccanum*;
the others, *O. pendulum*.

Fig. 33. The youngest prothallium that was found of *O. moluccanum*, x65, t, basal tuber; rh, rhizoids.

Figs. 34–42. Various forms of the prothallium of *O. pendulum* x3. Figs. 34, 40, 41, and 42, show the attached sporophyte. In Fig. 41, a rootlet, r, is developing from the primary root.

Fig. 43. A nearly median section through the apex of a young prothallium of *O. moluccanum*, x65. A two-celled embryo, em, is present.

Fig. 44. The apical region of the same x275.

Fig. 45. Longitudinal section through a portion of a large prothallium of *O. pendulum*, x25. The dotted areas show the distribution of the endophyte; ♂, empty antheridia.

Fig. 46. A cross-section of a branch of a similar prothallium, x25.

Fig. 47. Apical cell of a branch of the prothallium, in longitudinal section, x275.

Fig. 48. Unicellular hair from the surface of the prothallium of *O. pendulum*, x275.

PLATE XII.

Fig. 49. Section of the tuberous base of the prothallium of *O. moluccanum*, x65. ♂ an old antheridium.

Fig. 50. Outer cells of the tuber, showing the endophyte, x275.

Fig. 51. A rhizoid, showing penetration of the mycorhiza, x275.

Figs. 52, 53. Rhizoids from prothallium of *O. moluccanum*, x275.

Fig. 54. Transverse section of a pro-

thallial branch of *O. pendulum*, x65. ♂, antheridium; ♀ archegonium.

Fig. 55. Two cells from near the apex of a prothallial branch of *O. pendulum*, before the invasion of the endophyte, x480.

Figs. 56, 58. Cells infected by the endophyte, x275.

Figs. 59—61. Oögonium-like bodies of the endophyte, x480.

PLATE XIII.

Figs. 62, 63. Young antheridia of *O. moluccanum*; longitudinal sections, x480.

Figs. 64, 65. Two older antheridia, x275; o, opercular cell.

Fig. 66. An older antheridium; surface view, x275; o, opercular cell.

Fig. 67. Transverse section of the apex of a prothallial branch of *O. pendulum*, x275, x, the apical cell.

Fig. 68. Longitudinal section of the apex of a prothallial branch of the same species, showing the apical cell, x, and two young antheridia, x275.

Fig. 69. Longitudinal section passing through three nearly full-grown antheridia, x65.

Figs. 70–72. Young antheridia of *O. pendulum* in longitudinal section, x275.

PLATE XIV.

Figs. 73, 74. Young antheridia of *O. pendulum*, longitudinal sections, x275; in 73, the nuclei are dividing.

Figs. 75, 76. Two transverse sections of a young antheridium of *O. pen-

dulum*, x275. Fig. 75 shows the surface view.

Fig. 78. Surface view of a nearly full grown antheridium of the same species; o, the opercular cell, x274.

193

Fig. 79. Two spermatogenic cells of *O. moluccanum*, before the final division; bl. the two blepharoplasts; x950.

Figs. 80—83. Development of the spermatozoid in *O. moluccanum*, x950; Fig. 83 shows the separate blepharoplast with the cilia. In Fig. 80, b, the blepharoplast is shown in section.

Fig. 84. Spermatogenic cell of *O. pendulum* before the final division, x950.

Fig. 85. Last division in the spermatogenic cell, showing the very large nuclear spindle; bl, the blepharoplasts, x950.

Fig. 86. Transverse section of the nuclear plate, showing the very numerous chromosomes, x950.

Figs. 87—93. Development of the spermatozoid of *O. pendulum*, x950, bl, blepharoplast; c, cilia.

Fig. 94. Nucleus from a nearly mature spermatozoid, x950.

Fig. 95. Three spermatozoids from sections of open antheridia, x950; v, the cytoplasmic vesicle.

PLATE XV.

All figures of *O. pendulum*.

Fig. 96. Two spermatozoids from an open antheridium, material fixed with FLEMMING's solution; x950; bl, blepharoplast; n, nucleus; v, vesicle.

Fig. 97. Transverse section of the apex of a prothallial branch, x275, x, apical cell; ♀, young archegonium.

Figs. 98—108. Longitudinal sections, showing the development of the archegonium, x275; b, basal cell; n, neck canal cell; v, ventral canal cell.

Fig. 107, an archegonium with two neck canal cells.

Fig. 109. An open archegonium showing a spermatozoid within the neck canal.

Fig. 110. An oblique section through an archegonium, showing the recently formed ventral canal cell, v, x650.

Fig. 111. A similar section, the ventral canal cell somewhat distended; n, one of the neck canal cell nuclei; x650.

PLATE XVI.

Figs. 112, 113. Two longitudinal sections of old archegonia of *O moluccanum*, x275.

Fig. 114. Transverse section of the venter of a similar archegonium.

Fig. 115. Section of an archegonium of *O. pendulum*, which has just been fertilized; x275. A spermatozoid, sp, has penetrated the nucleus of the egg; other spermatozoids in the neck of the archegonium.

Fig. 116. Two-celled embryo of *O. moluccanum*; x275; ar, neck of archegonium.

Fig. 117. Nearly median longitudinal section of an older embryo of *O. pendulum*, x275. I—I, the basal wall; r, apical cell of root.

Fig. 118. Two transverse sections of a four-celled embryo, x275.

Fig. 119. Two oblique sections of a five-celled embryo, x275.

Fig. 120. Nearly median longitudinal section of an older embryo, x110: r, the root.

Figs. 121—123. Three transverse sections of an embryo of about the same age as the one shown in Fig. 120, x275.

PLATE XVII.

Fig. 124. Nearly median longitudinal section of an older embryo of *O. pendulum*, x65; r, the root.

Fig. 125. An older embryo of the same type, x65; f, foot; r², second root.

194

Fig. 126. The second root from the same, x110.

Fig. 127. Horizontal section of the second, or elongated type of embryo, x110. f, foot; r, root.

Fig. 128. Median section of the first type of embryo, after the roots have broken through the prothallium x25. The tracheary tissue is beginning to form, and the endophyte is established. The latter is indicated by the dotted area; r¹, r², first and second roots; f, foot; pr, prothallium.

Fig. 129. Longitudinal section of the young sporophyte of *O. moluccanum*, showing the cotyledon, l, and the base of the root, r, x65.

Fig. 131. Apex of the cotyledon from an older sporophyte x275. x, the apical cell.

Fig. 132. Longitudinal section of the young sporophyte of *O. moluccanum*, showing its relation to the prothallium, pr; x8.

Figs. 134, 135. Two forms of the fully developed lamina of the cotyledon of *O. moluccanum*, x5.

PLATE XVIII.

Fig. 135. Longitudinal section of the young sporophyte of *O. moluccanum*, x25; l, cotyledon; r, root; a bud, k, is forming at the apex of the root,; pr, prothallium.

Fig. 136. Middle region of the young sporophyte, x65.

Fig. 137. Bud, shown in Fig. 135, x110, r. root, apex.

Fig. 138. Transverse section of the apex of the primary root, x275.

Fig. 139. Transverse sections of primary root, back of the apex, x110.

Fig. 140. Vascular bundle of the primary root, x275

Fig. 141. Vascular bundle from the mid-region, x275.

Fig. 142. Transverse section of the petiole of the cotyledon, x65.

Fig. 143. Part of a tracheid from the middle region of the sporophyte, x480.

Fig. 144. Vascular bundle of the first root of *O. pendulum*, x110; en, endodermis.

Fig. 145. Longitudinal section of the young sporophyte of *O. moluccanum*, showing the adventitious bud, k, x65.

Fig. 146. Vascular bundle of the first root of the sporophyte, juct below the attachment of the bud, x275.

Fig. 147. Section of the young bud associated with the root shown in Fig. 146; st, stem-apex; l, first leaf.

Fig. 148. Transverse section of a slightly older bud, showing the apical cell of the stem, x.

PLATE XIX.

Fig. 149. Section of a bud on the first root of *O. moluccanum*, x10; l, leaf, st, stem-apex; sh, sheath about the stem-apex.

Fig 150. Section of an older bud, showing the first root of the bud, r¹, x65.

Fig. 151. Stem-apex of the bud shown in Fig. 150; x110.

Fig. 152. Middle region of a young sporophyte of *O. moluccanum* showing two leaves, x65.

Fig. 153. Adult sporophyte of the typical *O. moluccanum*, natural size.

Fig. 154. Small form of *O. moluccanum* (?) natural size.

Fig. 155. Two spores of the typical *O. moluccanum*, x480.

Fig. 156. Sculpturing of the spore-membrane, x950.

Fig. 157. Two spores of the large cordate leaved *O. moluccanum* (?), x480. These usually are bi-nucleate.

Fig. 158. Sculpturing of spore-membrane, x950.

Fig. 159. Very small spore of *O moluccanum* (?) x480.

Pl. IX.

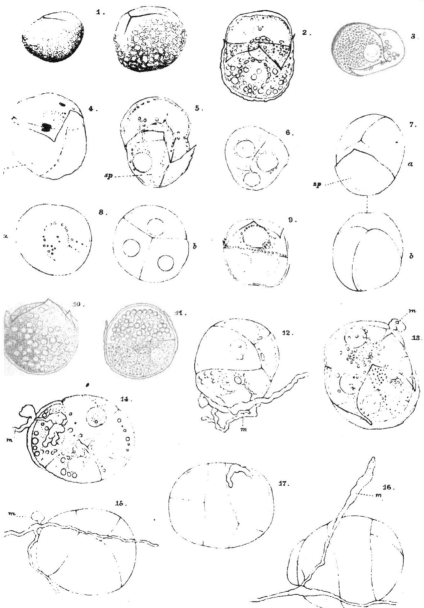

Pl. X.

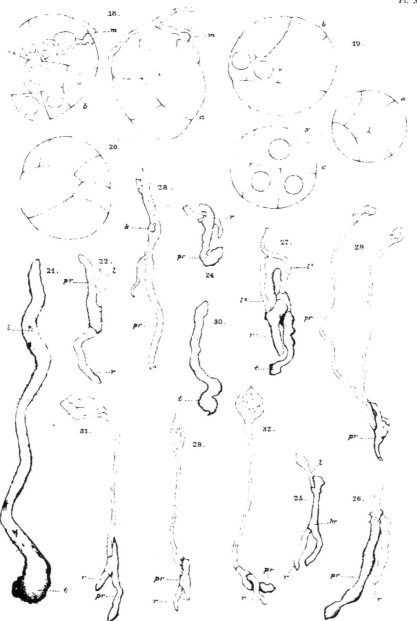

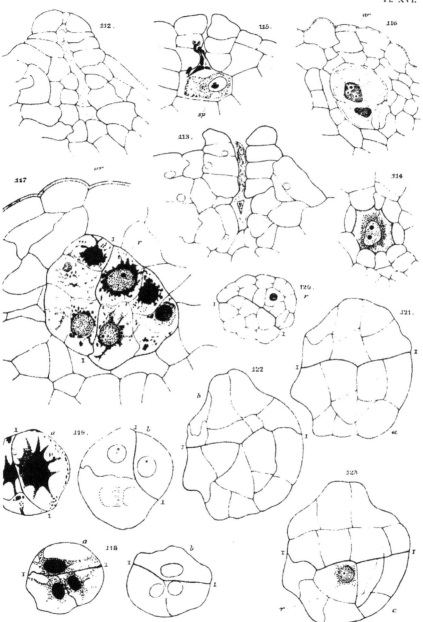

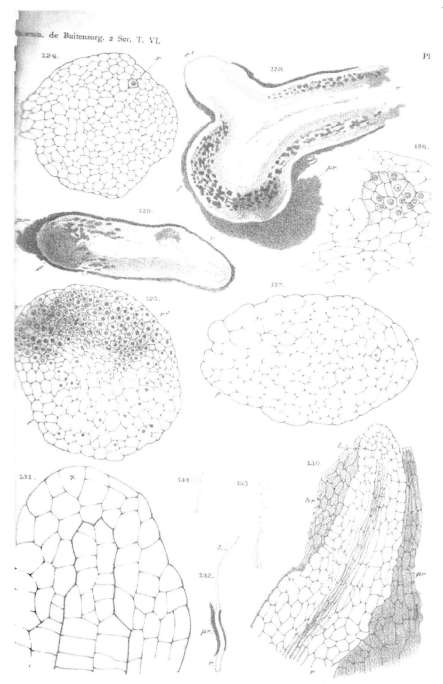

Pl. XVIII.

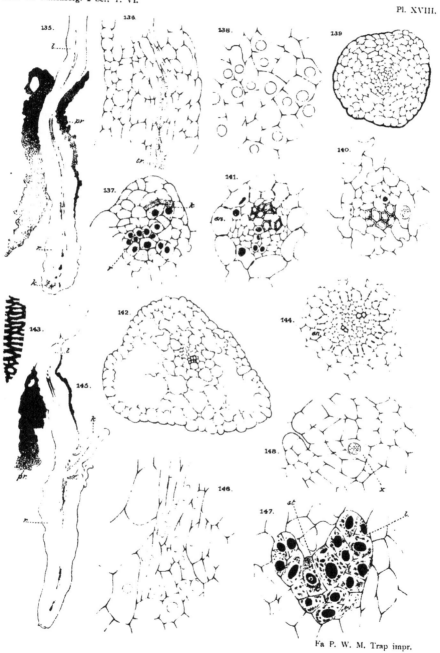

Fa P. W. M. Trap impr.

Pl. XIX.

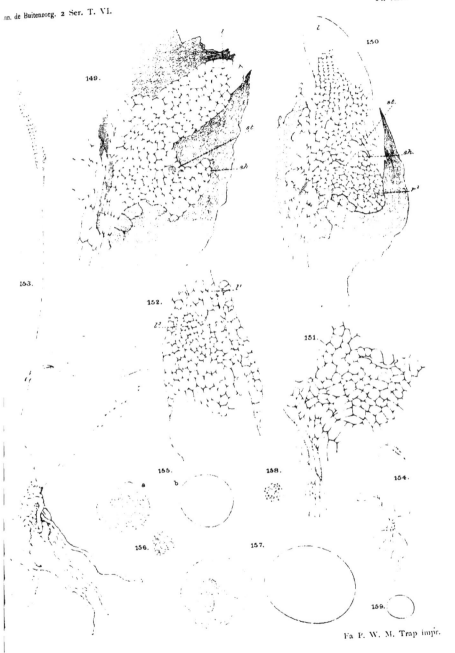

CPSIA information can be obtained
at www.ICGtesting.com
Printed in the USA
LVHW080746180121
676573LV00038B/124